Ramblings

A Poetry Collection

To Robert, who never understood my poetry but never stopped believing in me.
To my dad, who introduced me to poetry.
To my mom, who taught me how to write, when all I wanted to do was read.
To you, may your words reach far and wide, may you never stop searching.

Table of Content

-There is none, read in whatever order you like and let the words connect to you.

If Lips Could Speak

Rooms have been painted with silence

Forgotten words left unsaid

We are but the dead

The living like our regrets

Have gone on without us

Mercy, we pray

On mornings when the sun refuses to show its face

Our tears have never been so sweet

If lips could tell a tale so true

I would give my lips

Just to say I love you

Mourning; Grief

Hope

Hope dances on the wind

Whispering in a sweet soft voice on the darkest of

nights

When the world has gone cold

And there are no fires to scare away the night

Hope lingers on the lips of lovers

It clings to goodbyes as if they were not so

It wishes for tomorrow

Hope is a torturous friend

It snickers at your dreams

And tells you to come again

It is witty and wise

Holding on to the one thing you ever wanted

Hope lies within the confines of our own inability

For when we hope

We touch the sky and all that dwells therein

Hope is a masterful friend

Never offering enough

But always lingers just outside of your touch

It draws you in

Then turn its back

There is no greater pain than hope

Hope for tomorrow

Hope for change

Hope lingers just outside of the frame

Never close but always just yonder

It beckons you

Like a siren or a flute

Then drowns your soul in the things lest hoped for

Hope as a complicated emotion

I Will Be Waiting

My bones are old

This casket holds what's left of me

The dead don't need remembering

They don't need caring for neither

No one listens to the dead

Though we knock

Scream words of advice

"No don't go down that alley"

No one listens to the dead

March on to life

Make love to your wife

For she is lonely

Soon I will be gone

And all that could ever be remembered about me

I will fade from history

And my story will be forgotten

If I had one more thing to say

Goodbyes were never my strong suit

So instead, I'll see you on the other side

For now, I'll keep you company, my love

I will watch over you this time

And when you die

I'll be there to greet you

Like an old friend

Like a lover

With arms open wide to happily ever after

Being the "other woman" or "other lover"

The Coaxing of a Fae

Little girl

Listen to my voice

Take a jab at the old winding road

Come and join me

For I am oh so alone

No kin, nor company will come to call my own

Little girl

Listen to my voice

Come and play a jig for me

You may dance and spin

As much as you like

But when the clock strikes 12 you must take flight

For there are dangerous things

In the middle of the night

Things that might eat a little girl

All in one bite

You must come and visit me

On the morrow's full moon

Then we can sing together

In the depths of my tomb

Little girl

Be not afraid

I am just an old woman now

Yet an old maid

My skin has gone wrinkly

And my eyes are bad

So little girl visit me

When the nights have made me sad

When the skies begin to cry

And the earth has gone cold

Little girl

Listen to my voice

And lend me your soul

The power of youth over lonely
aged women (not a grandmother)

Come to me

In the night

When the birds have gone to sleep

Come to me

With open arms

Come to me

Before the dew has set

Come to me

In the morning before my first breath

Before my eyes greet the day

Bring me sweet kisses

On the morning's rays

Come to me

In the middle of the day

My heart beats for you

My love, my life

I wait for you

Heart in hand

Impatiently

My mind races to the moment when you arrive

My heart skips a beat

Oh my love

To see your face

My heart breaks

You are no longer mine

You have left me before the morning dew

My tears

They know no rest

A river flows from where my heart used to be

I am broken

I am lost

But still, I beg of thee

Come to me

Before the moon rises

Reclaim me once more

To put my heart at ease

Please my love

I beg of thee

Come to me

Mourning the loss of a
relationship

A Vendor's Complaint

T'matoes

T'matoes

For 6 cents and not a nickel more

Right off the vine

You can still smell the earth on 'em

"Hey pretty lady, won't you by some t'matoes for your family"

"No, I shan't. I have no more money to spend in this place"

"Me lady, I'll drop the price for ya"

"Oh"

"Just a nickel and this lovely bunch could be yours"

"No. it's still too much"

"Then be off with ya!"

"Scatt! Begone. Ya poor sack of bones"

I sell my product fair and square

Never going above the price

And when the poor folks come

I give them free rice

For all my hard work

I've never made a cent

And now they come to beg

My shop is open six days a week

And I still can't get a good price

My heart is in the right place

With all this debt I have to face

Straight-laced boots tied

I spend my days in the market

Trying to make a life

"I can't sell ya all me vegetables if it's not a fair price"

"I'll tell ya what, bake me a bread"

"Just like my mum used to make"

"And when you're done, I'll buy it for a fair sum"

"It will be a trade"

"Then you can be on your merry little way"

They barter and they beg

I have no choice but to give

I see those teary faces

And all my heart breaks in me

Call me a mush or what you like

These poor kids are starving into the night

They have no homes

No family to love

Call me a beggar

But I am doing the work

For the one above   God

And when my time comes

I'll make a deal

Strike it fair

My works for an entrance

And a gold perch

There I shall rest my days

In a stupor haze of delight

Thanking God for the trade

I made that night

The Market

Early in the morning

You can see them walking

Up the streets to the shops

They will gripe and bicker

Stomp their foot at the seller

All for a cent more

A sigh rises into the air

You can smell the despair

Now they come

One by one

To see what Mr. Turnike has to sell

You will watch him frown

As they talk his prices down

He will snap and snare

All to get a fair share

A tomato

Slides off his stall

Making its way down the street

In the hands of Little Timmy

His feet can only go so fast

As he dashes around the corner

Ready to make his move

"Thief"

THIEFFFFF"

His head dashes up

As his eyes search the crowd

Shoving the tomato into his mouth

Gobbling it down

He was almost caught

But not this time around

He walks on into the alley

Into the cold night

The market is quiet now

Not a stall in sight

All the milk was sold today

And the farmers had a crowd

The market is now closed

And the moon is high

A profit lost

A profit gained

In the market, it's all just the same

He Smelled Like Forever

He smelled like forever

As if forever could be measured by time

He smelled like an eternity

Of sunshine

Beautiful rain as it would seem

A subtle combination of uneasiness

That was his scent

He carried it like an old picture

Battered around the edges from his personal war

Against the phantom, he seemed to be

His fight was not for want or need

Rather for an identity, he sought

A recognition of sorts

He bled it

Wanted it badly

Like a dream that was never his reality

He smelled of fear and failure

As if success was too much to carry

He smelled of a long lost misery

As if the pain was his to bury

Maybe he smelled of comfort and familiarity

Beautiful wishes left unsaid

Broken promises

Dead on the sidewalk where his heart used to be

He smelled of mystery

Of a fragrance in time

He smelled like an eternity

And in all his failure he was mine

To love

To hold

To have

To behold

A thousand times he was mine

With cuts and bruises

Battered around the edges and all

A shy smile and a scent of wonder

He smelled like forever

And forever he was mine

Finding the love of one's life
Posession

Impermanent Thoughts

Impermanent thoughts

Described him best

Here one moment

And gone the next

He had a way with words

Like a swordsman but not

He wove them with his voice

Into crystal beings

His words stood up

And walked on their own

Just like yesterday

Like a whisper

Gone to the winds

If you heed it not

He was a man of many words

But only spoke when spoken to

Like a forgotten thought

He lingered on

The edge of your mind

You knew him

Loved him deeply

But he was a fleeting thought

Never yours to be tied down

By wants or love of any sort

He moved like the wind

Swiftly

Yet calmly he walked on

And just like a zephyr

He would move on

Impermanent in his existence

Like a flame

Put out before too long

Please Don't Tell Him the Truth

Tell him that you won't be coming home tonight

[Tell him that the bruises on his face are his fault]

Tell him not to make you angry

Tell him that you love him

But please don't tell him the truth

Don't tell him that you hate him

Don't tell that he deserves better than you

Don't tell him that you are broken

That your heart no longer knows what warmth is

Don't tell that the bottle is your only friend

Tell him that you are getting help

Tell him that you won't hit him again

Tell him all the lies you can

But please don't tell him the truth

Don't tell him that there is no redemption for you

Don't tell him that the nights are cold without him

Bleed

Break his heart

But please don't tell him the truth

A Witch's Farewell

In the morning

Before the sun rises

My love, you must leave me behind

Run to the hills on where the tulips grow in spring

There you will find a letter buried beneath the snow

It will be the last of its kind

For tonight I must pass on to another world

Run as far as you can

These people who were once our friends

Have turned their backs on us now

The snicker and whisper

In their houses, before the fire

As it crackles and pops through the night

They used to love us

Call us helpers

But now we are witches

Who must pay the cost

For the lives lost in this village

My child, you must run through the western forest

On the fourth night

After I have burned and left my curses

Go to the old tree and tell him your name

Learn the ways of those who were maimed

Take time my child

For you are the last of our kind

Fear not of the darkness that lingers still

And take not the drop of life

Seek not revenge

Lest it makes your heart evil

Live as we did with our heart in our hand

Take my last breath

As I wish you farewell

Let the light lead you

Through our darkest spell

And let your heart

Be good and pure

For only then shall you join me again

In a realm where not hate lives

And a den where the dawn greets the day.

The Wind

The wind laughs through the trees

It breezes by the lake

And runs to play in the meadow with Autumn's leaves

It whisp and swings on butterfly's wings

Whispering sweet giggles in the ears of young and old

It dances on the corner and tickles your nose

Pokes you as you come close

It shuffles in the streets

And marches to the beat

It skips across your top lip

And chuckles to itself

Climbing up the mountain

It reaches for air

And then blows the snow into the air

Knocking on windows and doors

It greets the morning while you still snore

It jumps to the windchimes and dances around

And when evening comes

It takes its rest on the ground

A day full of play has gone by

And the wind shall start again!

But not tonight

As it slides through the trees

Stretches its hands to the meadows

It waves farewell

It must now sleep a spell

Abandoned Town

There is a tapping on the wall

In the midnight hour

When the sun has gone to rest

And the moon bids you hello

There is a knocking at the door

When the pixies come to play

And the flowers have risen to meet the day

There is a whisper through the trees

When the lunch bell has rung

And the children have gone to play

There is a creaking in the woods

Where the old bridge used to be

And the pond used to lay

But now the town is empty

Not a sound to be heard

Not a pot to be stirred or a child to chide

Now the town is forgotten

As if it never were

Betrayal

Somewhere deep within I have already lost a friend

"It was just a game, " she said

A silly little crush of sorts

Crushed my heart to pieces

Take my soul away

Bury me beneath the love that I once had

And smile

Smile for the world to see what a friend you were to me

Smile to the blade in my back

A laugh rises in the air

Then disappear as if to play pretend

A cruel heart has your mind

And to the abyss, you go to find your soul

In the arms of the one you left behind

A friend lost

A lover gone

Take your time

Because when the doors close

And the reality sets in

The blade in my back is now your only friend

Take What is Left of Me

Take what is left of me

And give it to a friend

My heart was never mine to hold

Not even in the beginning

You carved it out

Of my chest

Wore it as a decoration

As you declared my love

Useless

Take my pride

And rip it to pieces

I am now a cruel woman

As life is a cruel mistress

So I shall walk these streets

Taking what was taken from me

My pride

My heart

My love

I shall claim them

In the sheets

In the back of cars

On the rooftops

I will yell to the heavens

"Take what is left of me"

For in return

Then I shall know

The love that hides deep within my soul

A love that knows no end

A love to my only God and friend

Depression

Tear stained cheeks

Tell a story that my heart can merely utter

The words have lost their way in my throat

The depression is eating me alive

Colors draining from the world around me

Irritation kicks in

Agitation takes its place

I am a lost child

Frustration has come to play

My heart beats fast

I am a disappointment

I know that I have failed

The voices tell me so

The pain is unbearable

I am angry

Yet Sad

What is this muddle of emotions?

I can't tell my guilt apart from my satisfaction

The lines run together

Separation no more

In this dark corner of my mind

I am a child

Scared of the dark and terrified of the light

It hurts this feeling of skin

Please rescue me from this mood I'm in

I can't think clear

Here in this dark corner

I am drowning

Yet swimming just the same

No hope looks for me

Despair has become my friend

And misery my company

A Father's Dreams

A mother's tears teach young girls to be sad

Because Dad was never the man you thought he was

He was never as sweet or as kind

He lost his love while searching for a dream he could

not remember

Father never loved like her like he did a dream

Maybe it was hope that killed him

Or the closed doors

Oh he how he would beat against them

Pleading to be let in

Just one more chance

One more time to get it right

One more yes

One more year to prove his worth

But dad, you were always my yes

Always so sweet

Harsh words don't mean the same when you are weak

You didn't mean it,

You never do

So dad go chase your dreams

Until they mean to you as much as I do

A Letter of Apology

I wanted to say I was sorry

Your words never hurt me

I forgive you

My bitterness has passed

died in its own grave

But each step closer brings me pain

I love you was never the same

Dark wounds don't heal

How was I supposed to know how you feel

Who was I to fix you

Yes I was bitter but Dad

You should have protected me

I would have known then that you loved me

Your words carry no merit

You don't mean it

I only see you through the past eyes

Fixed on your flaws

How was I to see different

How was I to know

That you wanted to change

Your ship has sailed

Your train has left you behind

Your words leave no comfort

I walk on eggshells in your leave

I do not trust myself to speak

I'll just tell you lies

I'll nod and smile

I am my own deceit

My own traitor

I forgive you

I no longer hate you

The only person I hate is

the one that looks back at me

When there is no one left to speak

I Have Left

I have saved a seat for you compliments

And left room for your kisses

A little sliver between my fingers

Is how much space I have left for you

I have left the door open

If you so choose to come in

Because the pieces of myself

Have no meaning with your absence

Raged hearts don't beat as fast as free birds fly

Your leaving is like heavy breathing

A sin of a sort

I seek forgiveness in your arms

On your lips

Yet empty hand greet me with cold eyes

No forgiveness for my sins

Only mourning lies in the morning

When empty sheets don't mean the same

A seat for your compliments

Have gone cold like your heart

My soul dies at the sight of your departure

Parting is no sweet sorrow

Only torture for tomorrow

I Won't Say I Love You

I won't say I love you

Not this time

I won't feel

The burden of my own affections

I won't utter those words

Whether by fear of rejection

Or lack of respect

I won't look you in the eyes

I won't say those words

Whether from fear

That my tears won't reach you

Or the simplicity of the fall

I won't fall this time

I won't look for you

Even if my heart beats

By some rhythm

Every time they utter your name

I won't return this time

I'll leave you

Just like you left me

Alone with my regrets

I'll walk away

And never come back

I won't stay

Your words

Mean nothing now

All I can hear is the breaking of a promise

All the lies

Even the sweet ones

Don't mean the same

When your heart has left you with

Even in the grave

I won't say goodbye

I won't speak

Not to you this time

You have already left me

And this world behind

I won't cry

Won't think

Won't feel

Even in this uncertainty

I won't say I love you

Not this time

I'll have the last words

Regardless of what I feel

I won't utter a word

When you're 6 feet deep.

A haircut

Mama said, " You need to get your hair done, Perry."

Yet I wouldn't dare

You see I have a fear of those long scissors

And the ladies with too much hair

Mama said, "Perry, that just won't do."

Yet, I didn't care

The hairdresser's nails were like clippers

And the gossip mill has too much to hear

Whether my hair goes up or down

Either way, I look like a clown

With my hair two directions

It's hard to find the nearest intersection

My hair eats combs and brushes too

It gets tangled

All the way down to my shoe

"I might as well cut it," I said to mama

But then what would I do.

Seems like there is not much left

After a 46 inch cut

A Bob, a bob will do.

Short and nice

No tangles on this side

But plenty on the rest

My hair is now like a nest

Where birds come to rest

Failure Has Failed Me

I used to love failure

Until it failed me one time too many

I was fine

Knew what to expect at the end

But then Failure decided

It was done with me

Things started going right

Or wrong

Depending on who tells it

Failure left me

Shoved me on the road to success

With its high expectations

And senior intimidation

Distraught

Was the best word to describe me

Failure

Was my friend

A kind comrade

In the army of uncertainty

I would slip and fall

Into utter despair

Then failure would call

And help me to fall just a little further than before

No hope

Had ever held my hand

I've only known defeat in the sand

My walls crumble

As my potential rises

Failure now

Then fail again

Failure is what happens when you have lost your only friend?

My Redemption

On rainy days

When the sun has gone away

Like a flower without water

I wilt

It may be my guilt that has made me this way

Forgiveness

Is something I can never earn

My redemption is at hand

All I seek is a salvation

Which saves me from myself

I wish to be whole again

To find the broken pieces

Which I lack within

I wish for the world to stop spinning

Not to leave me behind

Remember me

And Weep

Weep for the life lost

My salvation was so close

To being complete

If only I knew

What being whole was

Then my redemption

Would have meant more

Than just a child's daydream

Withered Dreams

Withered dreams lay at my feet

In puddles of hopeless dreams

When I step closer, they struggle away

As if I were a disease

I see them in the alleyways

And across the street

In empty shopping malls

Where two paths meet

And if I were to approach

They'll growl and hiss

At my slightest consideration

Withered dreams lay at my feet

Never drawing closer

Always out of reach

And if you were to greet them

You would have thought

They were dreams of beauty

And of truth

Yet they wither and slouch

Whether for lack of trying or of need

Withered dreams lay at my feet

With scorn and reproach, they regard me

As if it was not me who gave them life

Yet it was me who let them die

And now they lay withered at my feet

My regrets have a place to be

They have come home

Now a place to rest

My dreams have lost their way

They lay withered at my feet

Their flight is over

Now lies their defeat

The Regret

In the depths of my farewell

My regrets begin to rise

It was a silly joke

To think love was mine

For all the burden in time

Hope now lays in a casket

And I am still among the living

You left

In such a rush

As if tired of the living

Now you're decorated

In the flowers you hated

In a world full of contradictions

You were my favorite

And the one I detest

Now you lay

In the ground

What's fair in your absence

The beating heart beats no more

All that you have left me with

Is this regret

This burning ache in my chest

Haunted

My house is haunted by words left unsaid

Forgotten deeds are buried with the dead

In the night

I hear voices speaking

Mumbling along the walls

Fear grips me

Holding on tightly

I can hear them now

My past regrets

They wash over me

As if consuming me without my approval

They dance along the walls

Laughing in the night

There is a chuckle going up the winding stairs

In the night

When I have laid my regrets to bed

And cast my doubts away

The ghosts of things left unsaid

Lears at me

Picking through my lies

The words no longer exist

They have been buried with the dead

Feelings of a forgotten tragedy

What do these words mean to me

They hold no meaning

They feel no hurt

And this is why they haunt me

In their unending curse

When the Moon Dreams

When the moon sleeps

It dreams of things

That has no meaning

To the modern man

There are wounds on its soul

That is older than the fragrance of time

The moon dreams

Of the past

Of things long gone

And memories best left alone

It is a lonely moment

Where the current ideas

Do not take hold

It dreams of old friends and forgotten lovers

Of revolutions long passed away

Of planetary motions

That has no meaning to its existence

It dreams

Darkness takes its soul

The other half still knows

The significance of the night

And if it were

To open its eyes

For just a moment or two

It would see

That dreams

Are no less than make belief

That its ideals

Mean nothing to a forgotten cause

For when it remembers

To close its eyes once more

It will fade

Into the night's sky

As if the universe

Reclaimed what it once lost.

To Sing and Dance in the Macabre Parade

There are musicians in the streets

A parade they say

Oh the crown has won the day

Our country is now at peace

No need for enemies

We can relax and play

We can sing and dance in the Macabre parade

Oh what a day

What a night

We can sing until the moon has lost its light

We will pray

For peace ever more

To sing and dance in Macabre parade

The dead shall rise

All dressed up

To sing and dance and run amuck

Oh what a sight

What a joy

When morning comes

We will sing once more

Cheers to the crown

And peace forever more

Our honor and our king

You never let us down

Long live the crown

A Dance of the Night

To seduce the light

She dances

On the heels of time

She reaches for a sky

That has already left her

Alone in the darkness

Now she breathes in the night

As if to hold it close

It claims her as its own

So she dances

On the edge of time

One foot at a time

As a beacon

To the lost souls

Who runs to her

Seeking a salvation

She can never truly give

So she dances

Again

And again

Until she is no longer on this plane of reality

Gone from the earth

She has fled

Dancing for the heavens to see

Her seduction

Has won

The heart of a love less permanent

Than the wrinkles of time

My fickle being

She dances in the Night

She dances in the night

As the light caress her hips

She is a vixen

Venom

Poison

She breathes in the night air

She is alive

Lungs filled with life

The tears stain her cheeks

Her voice won't speak

She dances just like she fights

Flowing like water

Continuous motion

She breathes in the night air

Her voice rises to meet the sky

She screams and shouts

She is the poison I seek

My lady, so beautiful to me

My heart races towards her

She is a vixen

A vision

A Celebration of motion

My goddess, my queen

I pledge my honor to thee

Beneath the House

In a box

Beneath the house on 5th street

Lives a little girl

About yea high

She can hardly speak

Never has she known love

Or the warmth of a hug

She cries at night

Beneath the house

There is a whimper

Louder than a mouse

And when she sees the light of day

She does not understand

Why something so warm feels empty

For she knows what the light means

One more night of screams

One more night of fear

One more night of her own tears

Running down her cheeks

Beneath the house on 5th Street

There lives a girl

About yea high

Doubt

Teardrops fall like rain on her cheeks

She is ill-content at the life she seeks

There is no happiness

In the little moments, she finds rest

She can not go on

Doubt clouds her mind

No Certainty

Can undo her disbelief

She has lost her faith

To one less than herself

And in the night she cries for help

Her voice reaches the heavens

And floats to the clouds

Yet her doubt keeps her grounded as if there were no
way out

She cries and begs for forgiveness

One as lowly as her

Tears stain her face

Yet she bows, for years in the same place

Her knees have gone cold

Mumbled words come from her mouth

The line between praying and begging

Has long been crossed

Her unanswered prayers

Make her crown

And in her doubt, she drowns

Uneasy

Gasping for air

She drowns weighed down

By her own disbelief

That life was never hers to seize

A Plain of Make Belief

There are marks down her arms

Scars where the skin used to be

Her wrists don't work anymore

She is bruised

Screaming

The pain is beyond anything she knows

She is lost

Dreaming

Her voice won't breach the church walls

She calls for God

But her ears have gone deaf

She can't hear his voice telling her to rest

She begs

And pleads

But no one hears her call

Her voice won't reach

She is dying

She is the wounded child

The forgotten daughter

The abused lover

She is the broken

Into pieces no longer resembling a soul

Her heart breaks as she screams her last goodbye

Before she closes her eyes

A hand reaches out and holds her close

She is barely breathing

Only hope holds her here

A soul yet decease

Pleading

She lingers still

On the plain of make belief

Forever suspended in the uncertainty that hope brings

Words Left Unsaid

Little raindrops linger on the crown of my head

I spent my last moments listening to the dead

"Take a dive," they said

It won't hurt at all

They pull

And Tug

At my will for life

It's the antithesis of strife

Stifle my words

With hymns from the grave

Tuck away

My name

Their soul has lost its purpose

Now wandering in the abyss

The dead requests company

They'll drag you down

To the depths of your depression

And take your crown

Listen not

To their call

Heed not their words

Close your eyes

For as long as you need

Take this word from me

For the dead

Can only warn you

Of their own failure

I've spent my last moments listening to dead

Angry cries in the night

Dangerous words take flight

Your regret

Can only lay on the shelf you desire

Raise it higher

Lest you forget

Take your time

Don't listen to dead

Because words left unsaid

Carries their own regret

To the grave

Then in the silence of an eternity

They yell

Full of hate

Angry words

Shuffle into the darkness

Of an eternity

Of ambiguous uncertainty

A New Day

Take your time

And breathe in

Let your worries float away

Look to the sky

And say amen

For today is a new day

Cast your doubts aside

And walk in the light

Take a moment

And breathe in

The dawn has come

And dusk will soon be here

Use your time wisely

Have no regrets

Live your life

To your absolute best

Take pride

In your stride

And go on ahead

Believe in yourself

And when life gets hard

Believe in your heart

That these little struggles

Will all make sense

Breathe in

And let go

Be present with those here

And not with those below

Take a step

Moving forward yet

Still, we go

Drifting

Together, we tied the knot

With our blood, sweat, and tears

Our fears brought us to the brink

Of our lies

Our bond is broken on the hourglass of time

Wishing to go back to a time

Where our love was beyond who we thought ourselves

to be

Evolving

Changing

Moving to a place

Where we no longer know how to speak simple words

I love you does not roll off the tongue

We are now small planets

Revolving around each other

Silent greetings

Obligations

No feelings

Just waiting

For the simple words to be as powerful

As they once were

A Couple's Fight

Arms open wide

Tell me is this where we collide

Words fly from my mouth

Voices raised

A motion, a shout

Tell me is this where we fight

What a sight to see

My eyes have gone blind

My heart now cold

The door creaks

As you leave without looking back

Arms open wide

A place for you to return

Tell me is this where we bleed

All our desire start to kindle

A fire is born

Explosion

Arms open wide

Tell me is this where we die

Side by side

With words lost in our throat

A silence clings to the air

Our life my love

It has never been fair

His Need

He needed failure

Like he needed air

It was the only thing keeping him alive

His past was laden with forgotten pleasure

Of his desire

His soul was a run-down car

In need of everything

While rejecting it all the same

He was tired

Tired of the hope

And Lies

Tired that his failure

Had not led to his demise

He wanted it all to end

To bid success goodbye

He needed failure

So that he could keep the hope alive

Contradictory in nature

That was his purpose

To fail

And fail again

While trying so hard to succeed

The rejection

Fed his insanity

Made him believe

That his own depravity

Was all he could afford

Taking moments

That seemed so pure

And rejecting the innocence

Of his past remorse

His desire

Was to be nothing

So that pity would carry him

Sympathy would be his friend

Good vibes

Would come his way

So he worked to fail

And in his failure

He finally found success

Pretend

In the back of my mind

I can hear the words forming

"I am fine"

A smile appears on my face

Then a wince

And yet

I still pretend

I am not in pain

There is no wrong here

"I am fine"

"I am fine"

But I'm not

My nerves are on fire

And I am crying

Begging to be freed

From this pain

That claims me whole

Takes my very soul

And destroys all that I am

I am not fine

I can not be

The words form in my throat

But I refuse them

I won't say them

I won't utter a word

I will keep it to myself

And pretend with a smile

"I am fine"

While my insides burn

And the rage builds

Teeth gritted

Fist clenched

"I am fine"

To the very end

Let's play pretend

Hope for Tomorrow

I look for the light

Crave for it

My thoughts have been derailed

The train has lost its course

This worry I feel

I wear it like a second skin

Closer to me than a kin

I am sinking

Dying

Drowning

Destitute and alone

Waiting for the medication to kick in

My hands have begun to shake

Murmurs rise from my throat now

The doubt sets in

Did I do it right?

My heart starts to race

Dying

Drowning

Destitute and alone

The feelings don't change

My soul is crying

Please help me, for I am lost

I am scared of the dark

It clings to me

Claws at my heart

The little light I have left

Can not survive through the night

When dawn comes

Will the darkness leave me?

Will the light return?

Will hope find its way back to me?

Will my heart once more know of truth and not despair?

My little light will lead me to the dawn

My redemption is at hand

I must hope on tomorrow's present

My Precious Gift

The moon has risen

And my little one you should be asleep

Put your book away

Words can wait another day

Now close your eyes

And count to 10

Remember how warm a hug feels

Think of your favorite toy

Sounds of your little breath fill the air

Rest now my child

Listen to this sweet lullaby

And when you wake

The sun will rise

And greet you with a warm smile

You will rub your little eyes

And start the day again

And you will play

All day long

With a bounce in your step

Remember to clean your toys up

Before you take a nap

And as you wake

This time I will take

That curly head of yours and give you a kiss

My sweet little child

My precious gift

Mother's Love

Lonely Pondering

A lonely soul plays pretend

She hadn't left

No real surprise

All night had been her imagination

The flowers were long dead as well as he was

I'm his grave, his body lay and now he's idolized

Ohh he was kind

Of a fool

And he was a good (for nothing) an honest man

And he really loved his (other) woman

Such a guy

Such a guy….

But he isn't dead

As his body lay next to mine

It seems cold this time of night

There is no warmth between us.

I only wish he was dead

Yet I play pretend

A good wife I am

So cautious and kind

I've planned his death and paid my respects

And now… But just for now.

I'll be an honest lonely without an end.

Until then, I'll play pretend

About the Author

Joy is the last of four children with an imagination that is well beyond her years. She is highly uncomfortable writing in third person but it is a burden she is willing to bear.

She is married to an amazing human being with no children in the southern state of Georgia. Currently, she struggles with Fibromyalgia and would love to eat chocolate all day but that doesn't stop her from spending entirely too much time reading manga, talking to people on twitter, and making fun of her brothers.

When she isn't writing you can find her procrastinating in the kitchen or laying in bed waiting for the flare-up to pass.

She wanted me to tell you that...

"I am humbled that you have decided to buy my first book. I hope my writing inspires you to dream and make a world of your own"

Made in the
USA
Monee, IL